What others are saying about the *Together Forever: God's Design for Marriage* premarital counseling program

Pastors and churches who marry or minister to couples have a responsibility to do everything they can to ensure the long-term success, survival, and sanctity of the marriage covenant. That is the exact reason why I do not marry a couple unless they have been through *Together Forever* and why our church has installed it as a pillar of pastoral care along with *Putting the "Happily" Into Your Ever After* for already married couples. You simply cannot beat the combination of a trained Marriage By God mentor couple interactively processing the curriculum with a prospective or struggling couple. Every church that wants integrity in its couples or marriage ministry would serve its members and community well by installing Marriage By God.

> **Kenny Luck**, pastor at Crossline Community Church, award-winning author, founder of Every Man Ministries

In addition to the *Together Forever: Premarital Counseling Workbook,* Ed and Angie Wright have enabled you who serve as mentors and disciplers to succeed by following the easy-to-do steps in mentoring. The *Together Forever: Premarital Counseling Mentor's Guide* helps you anticipate reactions from the couple you mentor and be prepared and prayed-up to graciously encourage, guide, and respond. This will be a great asset to help you be prepared to contribute to a great marriage in the making.

> **Dr. Harold J. Sala**, founder of Guidelines International, author

Practical! That is the word that came to mind as I read Ed and Angie Wright's *Together Forever* premarital counseling mentor's guide. Their easy-to-follow guide helps direct the counseling couple who wants to assist other couples in maximizing their relationship and avoiding the pitfalls that so easily trip up the new bride and groom. As you read the guide, you'll say to yourself, "I can do that!"

> **Darlene Sala**, author, seminar speaker

As proclaimed in the name of their ministry, Marriage by God, Ed and Angie Wright's *Together Forever* premarital counseling workbook and mentor's guide are essential for training up engaged couples that seek to fulfill God's purpose in their marriage. Their mentor's guide reveals that not many should become teachers because God holds them to a higher standard. The Wrights represent the highest expression for God's intent for married couples and I wholeheartedly endorse without reservation these two excellent books.

> **Willie Naulls**, pastor, author

Very subtle changes from the earlier version of these materials have taken this mentoring program from good to great! We love it, and the Twenty-One Questions are a great addition to use as a quick reference in fine-tuning a couple's relationship.

Harold K. Webber, pastor of Living Way Christian Fellowship
Chester & Cheryl Young, directors of Marriage Enrichment

Ed and Angie Wright have beautifully put together a guide for both engaged couples as well as mentor couples. The guide is rich with spiritual and practical insights, with the end goal being for the engaged couple to be intentional about their marriage. The Wrights have given the whys behind intentionality as well as the practical tools and steps to make an intentional marriage possible. With humility and grace, the material is presented in a systematic, easy-to-follow weekly format. A fabulous resource in a world that is desperate for such content!

Kim Moeller, Christian author and speaker

Ed and Angie Wright have written a beautiful and biblical book on helping pre-married couples understand the full beauty of God's plan for marriage. They masterfully weave personal stories and insights to illustrate the elements of a biblical marriage that are completely practical. I highly recommend this resource for those that are mentoring couples considering marriage.

Carl Moeller, CEO Biblica-The International Bible Society

TOGETHER

Forever

GOD'S DESIGN FOR MARRIAGE

PREMARITAL COUNSELING MENTOR'S GUIDE

ED + ANGIE WRIGHT

MARRIAGE BY GOD

MARRIAGE BY GOD is a ministry of Guidelines International Ministries,
Mission Viejo, California

Together Forever: God's Design for Marriage; Premarital Counseling Mentor's Guide
Copyright © 2003, 2015, 2017 by Ed Wright.

Originally published as *Two Becoming One: Premarital Counselor's Guide*

Request for information or comments should be emailed to Angie@MarriagebyGOD.org.

We wish to dedicate this book to the Marriage by God mentor couples who have come beside us with a passion to help couples learn what it looks like to put Christ at the center of their marriage. You have humbly accepted God's assignment, and it has been exciting watching the Holy Spirit work in and through you as you pour blessings into the lives of couples preparing for marriage.

⁊⁊

Andy & Debby Benis
Dan & Carol Bobke
Todd & Moshelle Carlson
Keith & Debbie Hamilton
Brian & Jan Healy
Bob & Colleen Heineman
Mike & Nora Higa
Ken & Carol Holloway
Dwight & Catherine Mansfield
Brian & Colleen Myers
Mitch & Debbie Needelman
Alan & Patti Peviani
Fadi & Jane Ramadan
Tom & Kellie Richter
Ron & Darla Schreiber
Hans & Tina Schroeder
Jeff & Tiffany Thompson
Bill & Terri Van Workum
Jay & Cathryn Wade
Dave & Shannon Welsh

Special Thanks

A big thank you to Jean E Jones. You embraced our vision with care as you gave heartfelt attention to every detail in critiquing, editing, and formatting our materials.

Contents

Introduction to Premarital Counseling

As iron sharpens iron, so one man sharpens
another.—Proverbs 27:17

Overview of the Program

Congratulations on your decision to become a mentor couple to engaged couples. You have been selected because you expressed an interest in the ministry and appear to be living a joy-filled, Christ-centered, long-term marriage (ideally ten years or more).

Marriage is tough. There is no way around it. However, with the proper biblical principles and the loving guidance of Christian mentors, the institution of marriage becomes the rich blessing God intended it to be. This program is designed to show engaged couples how to live out God's design for marriage in order to be together forever. Throughout the process, you, as mentors, will share biblical principles and time-tested techniques for fulfilling God's great plan for marriage.

Your goal as a mentor couple is not to solve your couple's problems, but to equip them with the tools needed for them to solve their own problems. As is often said, "Give a man a fish; you feed him for a day. Teach a man to fish; and you feed him for a lifetime."

This program is designed for you to meet with your couple for six sessions to guide them through the materials. In preparation for each session, the engaged couple will read the three chapters that make up each session and answer the corresponding questions. Each one is to complete his or her homework alone. They will be asked not to share their answers before they come together for their session. This allows for truth and spontaneity to come out during the sessions. It also allows for much more successful, open-minded mentoring sessions.

At each session, you, the mentoring couple, will lead the couple through each chapter as they share their answers with each other. You will be there to encourage, inspire, and affirm the couple in their areas of strength. You will also be there to share openly and honestly with the couple from the wealth of knowledge and experience gained from your own Christ-centered marriage. The notes in your counselor's guide will help you educate the couple on key principles and tools that will aid them in having a strong marriage in Christ. It is your job to be there with guidance to challenge and motivate the couple to make appropriate changes in their areas that need strengthening.

Studies show that the happiest people in the world are married. Unfortunately, studies also show that the unhappiest people in the world are married. As you can see, the stakes are high. When couples learn God's blueprint for marriage, the institution of marriage becomes the rich blessing God intended it to be.

Remember these important points when mentoring a couple:

o   Be open and honest with your couple and encourage them to be the same.

o   Assure your couple that you will keep all information they share confidential.

o   Be exceptional listeners.

o   Be more interested than interesting. Try to listen at least 70 percent and talk no more than 30 percent. Remember, this is your couple's time to grow together.

o   Show them through your facial expressions and your eye contact that you are listening and interested in what they are saying.

o   Be careful not to express any feelings of judgment or disapproval.

o   One of the great values of mentoring couple-to-couple is that men and women sense things differently. If you intuitively sense there is more to someone's answer than what they've spoken, try to draw out their feelings by saying, "Tell me more," or asking open-ended questions such as, "I sense there is a little more that you have to say on this. Will you elaborate?" This is especially important on topics that are difficult for them to discuss.

o   Use statements like, "What do you think about what your fiancé just shared?" or "Explain a little more about what you are trying to say."

o   Give loving guidance that is consistent with God's principles and Word.

o   Share helpful insights when appropriate.

o   Be aware of what your couple is saying, not only through words, but also through body language.

You will walk beside your couple, giving them the unconditional love of God by listening, remaining nonjudgmental, and sharing wisdom. The confidential, open, and trusting relationship with you will allow your couple to talk through important issues in their relationship, and even explore areas that the couple may have avoided. Every couple will have issues exposed. Help and encourage them to grow in their areas of weakness or insecurity. Affirm them in their areas of strength.

Although this program is designed to be a "wellness care" program, at times issues may be exposed that require extra time and attention. In rare instances, a serious area of concern may expose itself (abuse, addiction, intense anger, infidelity, etc.). Immediately bring this to the attention of the ministry leader or pastor.

The Gift Goes On

While this program is designed to help engaged couples, there is also an incredible bonus for you, the mentoring couple. Coaching couples will strengthen your own marriage. As you instruct about God's design for marriage, you will grow in your understanding of living a Christ-centered marriage. You will also find yourselves sharing these principles and techniques with others, which will encourage their growth toward having Christ-centered relationships. Ultimately this program will help each couple involved grow in their love for one another, and grow deeper in their love for God. They will live out the greatest commandments of all: to love God and love others. That's proof again that you cannot out-give God!

Session I

Before You Meet

Review the three chapters in the *Together Forever: God's Design for Marriage; Premarital Counseling Workbook* that you will be covering tonight with your couple so that you are familiar with the session content. Your goals for the first session will be to:

o   Get to know your couple and set the stage for open and honest discussion.
o   Be a good listener.
o   Be alert to your couple's body language, which often communicates more to you than the words they speak.
o   Begin identifying your couple's strengths.
o   Begin identifying your couple's areas of needed growth.

Identifying your couple's strengths and desired growth areas will allow you to customize the mentoring program to your couple's needs. When your couple is strong in an area, don't spend too much time on those questions. When your couple exposes an area that needs attention, feel free to give an extra homework assignment to help them grow in that area.

If you find either one or both individuals giving brief answers to the questions, give a pregnant pause after they finish. This will hopefully prompt them to expand on their answer. Don't be afraid to allow for times of silence. Remember, the success of the mentoring is based on their willingness to communicate openly and honestly with each other.

Here are a few additional notes before you start:

o   The questions from the workbook are in bold print.
o   Have the woman answer the odd questions first, and have the man answer the even questions first, thus alternating back and forth.
o   The mentor notes are written so that you can, if you would like, read the information to your couple, although we recommend trying to be familiar enough with the material that your discussions flow freely.

CHAPTER 1

Two Becoming One

1. **Give at least three advantages to being married over being single.**

   There are many advantages to being married over being single. Some of the benefits are companionship, emotional support, physical intimacy, the possibility of building a family, and sharing life experiences together. It is special to have someone who is on your team, cheering your successes, encouraging you through your challenges, supporting you in your sorrows, and loving you no matter what.

2. **What would you like to see God accomplish through this premarital counseling program? Be specific.**

   This gives all of us an idea of what you are expecting to accomplish. Do you each agree with what your partner answered?

3. **Have you had a breakup anytime since you became exclusive? If so, what was the reason?**

   It is not uncommon for a couple to break-up once during their courtship. In fact, it can actually be healthy. A break-up can strengthen your resolve that you cannot see yourself going through life without your fiancé. It can help you work towards strengthening your love and commitment. However, if there have been repeated break-ups, this can be evidence that you have some negative relationship patterns that need to be broken for the health of your relationship. We will be sharing numerous skill sets to help you resolve conflict and differences in a healthy manner.

4. **How do you feel about divorce?**

Understanding what the Bible says about divorce is important. There are two key verses that show us God's attitude towards divorce. Malachi 2:16 states, "I hate divorce, says the LORD God of Israel." Matthew 19:6 says, "...so they are no longer two, but one. Therefore what God has joined together, let man not separate."

Although the Bible allows for divorce in certain situations (such as infidelity), divorce should never be considered the best option. Couples should always consider reconciliation as their first option. Couples who consider divorce a viable option more easily consider it when their marriage undergoes stress or becomes unsatisfactory to one or to both partners.

Not only should divorce not be an option, you should make a pact with each other that you will never threaten divorce as a means to hurt or create an impact.

5. **On a scale of 1 to 10, rate your compatibility in the seven areas below.**

1 = not compatible at all
10 = extremely compatible

Factor	Rating
Fun	
Friendship	
Finance	
Family	
Forgiveness	
Future	
Faith	

- Do you have any questions on chapter one?

CHAPTER 2

Love Spoken Here

1. **Which of the three types of love needs the most growth in your relationship (eros, philia, or agape)?**

   Keeping all three types of love alive in our relationship is important. We can easily become lazy or complacent in one or more areas if we're not careful.

   The most important thing to a woman is to be cherished by her man. The best way to cherish her is to show her and others how special she is to you.

   A man's greatest desire is to be respected by the woman in his life. The best way to respect your man is to be his biggest fan. This should be done privately and publically.

2. **How often does your fiancé tell you that he or she loves you?**

   You may not have grown up hearing the words, "I love you," and you may be uncomfortable speaking them, but it's vital that you learn to tell your partner frequently that you love him or her. Keeping the love alive is essential. Take advantage of special moments with your future spouse to give a big hug or an extra-long kiss. Speak the words "I love you" daily. These simple gestures will keep love present in your marriage.

   Better yet, a study conducted by the National Communication Association found that hearing "I love you" from your loved ones actually lowers stress!

3. **If you were having a bad day, how could you avoid taking it out on your fiancé?**

First and foremost, pray! Then talk with your fiancé in a healthy way. Tell your future spouse what is really bothering you; for example, "I missed my dental appointment today" or "I have so much work to catch up on, I feel overwhelmed and frustrated."

You can also practice the art of "acting your way into a feeling." This means that even though your day is going bad, act and respond the way you would if you were having one of your best days ever. Eventually, the bad-day feelings will become less significant and you will probably start having a better day.

4. **Review the passage on love in 1 Corinthians 13:4–8. Which of the actions described in this passage may be challenging for you to show your fiancé? Why?**

The beauty of Christianity is learning to love as God loves. Few situations test this as radically as marriage. How easy it is to feel overwhelmed by the Apostle Paul's definition of love. It is impossible to demonstrate perfect love all of the time to our partner, but as we receive God's love, we can love our mate with the overflow of God's love. God's love will allow you to communicate love to your fiancé in a consistent, creative, and uninhibited way. The bonus is that others will notice and God will be honored!

5. **List ten things you love about your fiancé.**

Keep this list available and refer to it often. You may even want to have it read at your wedding ceremony. Whenever you become discouraged about your relationship, re-read the list of things you wrote that you love about your fiancé. One of the most effective tools for overcoming marital disappointment is replacing a negative thought about your husband or wife with a positive thought (such as those on the list of all of the things you love about your partner). Studies show that we can focus on only one emotion at a time: choose love.

- Do you have any questions on chapter two?

CHAPTER 3

The Freedom of Forgiveness

1. Why is it important to forgive your fiancé?

It is important for you to forgive because forgiveness is foundational to our whole Christian belief system. God loved us so much that He sent His Son to die for the forgiveness of our sins. God wants us to receive His forgiveness and to forgive as He forgave us. Colossians 3:13 tells us, "Bear with each other and forgive whatever grievances you may have against one another. Forgive as the Lord forgave you."

The Greek word for forgive is *charizomai*, which means, "to show grace or grant a pardon." Even if you haven't experienced the need to forgive your partner for very much at this point in your relationship, marriage is the union of two imperfect people whose faults will be exposed due to the intimacy of the relationship. A successful marriage will cultivate the attitude of forgiveness that Christ models.

2. How do you forgive someone you are having trouble forgiving, and how do you know you have forgiven them?

We forgive by faith, out of obedience to God. God wants us to love others and to love Him. This love He speaks of is a choice, not a feeling. We must trust God to complete His work in us. Make it between you and

God and not between you and the other person. Turn your heart over to God.

Corrie ten Boom, a Christian who survived a Nazi concentration camp, said that forgiveness is the key that unlocks the door of resentment and the handcuffs of hatred. It is a power that breaks the chains of bitterness and the shackles of selfishness.

When you forgive someone, you no longer want to hurt him or her with your words or actions. You aren't bitter about the issue that hurt you. One of the most loving actions you can continually take is forgiving.

3. **When you forgive someone, must you also trust them?**

Forgiveness and trust are completely separate. Forgiveness is something you give to another person. Trust is something they must earn back. God calls us to forgive those who have wronged us immediately— but this does *not* mean that we must immediately trust them. When there has been a breach of trust that requires forgiveness, it may take some additional time for the trust to be fully restored. Trust is something that must be earned back—through consistent accountability and time. As you read in the chapter, Joseph immediately forgave his brothers and even understood the bigger picture that what his brothers had meant for evil, God had used for good. But Joseph tested his brothers before he trusted them.

God wants us to forgive often and freely, but sometimes when trust has been broken, it is appropriate to establish boundaries until trust is earned back. Understanding the distinction between forgiveness and trust is important.

4. **Is there anyone in your life you need to forgive, or whom you need to have forgive you? What is preventing the forgiveness from taking place?**

Some find it difficult to forgive; others find it difficult to ask for forgiveness. What is standing in the way of your forgiveness issue? When you don't clear up areas of forgiveness in your life, you allow them to occupy negative space in your mind.

Not forgiving is like taking poison, thinking it is going to hurt the other person. Take your hurting heart to the Lord and ask for his help in forgiving.

Often, healing can be achieved through writing a well-worded letter (be careful not to include negative tag-ons). Sometimes it can be accomplished by simply giving the person a hug and asking, "Can we start over?" Turn to God, the Author of forgiveness, for your strength and peace. There is freedom in forgiveness!

- Do you have any questions on chapter three?

Closing Comments

- Ask your couple if they are willing to make a premarital covenant to stay sexually pure until their wedding night. If so, tell them you will help hold them accountable by asking them each week.

- Set up a time for your next session.

- Close in prayer.

Session II

Before You Meet

Depending on your couple's spiritual maturity, you may ask one (or both) to close your session in prayer. If you detect they may be hesitant or embarrassed, then you or your spouse should take the lead.

The main emphasis in Session II is for the couple to understand the importance of putting Christ at the center of their relationship. They will discuss how well they feel their fiancé is fulfilling their needs. Finally, they'll discuss how they view their future marital roles.

Here are some additional tips:

o   Encourage your couple to direct their answers towards each other and not to you. This will allow you to observe their reactions and interactions with each other. If you perceive negative or extreme responses, have each person comment and clarify their thoughts and feelings. Ask them to share what they thought of their partner's answer. Allow discussion to continue as long as the conversation moves in a positive direction. If the discussion leads to a conflict that cannot be resolved at that moment, move on to the next question. Explain that they will learn a process in Session IV that will help them resolve conflict.

o   If either individual did not complete all of his or her homework, remind them that completing the homework is crucial to the success of their premarital counseling experience. Completing their homework is an indication of their commitment to their marriage.

o   During the week, you may wish to email reminders and words of encouragement to your couple. The husband should email the man, and the wife should email the woman.

o   Each week it is important that you read the mentor's notes for each of the three chapters so you understand each question's purpose in the chapter. In addition, it is essential for you to be familiar with the chapter content in the couple's workbook for the three chapters you will be covering during the session.

CHAPTER 4

Putting Christ at the Center of Your Marriage

- Ask your couple if they have been faithful to their premarital covenant.

1. **Have you put Christ at the center of your life? If so, how?**

   When you put Christ at the center of your life, you allow God to direct all of your decisions and actions. It means you have a vibrant, on-going, daily relationship with God the Provider of all things. You recognize God as your Creator, Savior, and Lord of your life. It also means that you seek to glorify him in every aspect of your life—especially in your marriage.

2. *Wife-to-be only:* **What does submission to your future husband in a Christ-centered marriage mean to you?**

   Husband-to-be only: **What does loving your future wife as Christ loved the Church mean to you?**

   Mentor note: Have the wife-to-be and husband-to-be answer question 1, and then review Appendices 1 and 2 in their workbooks with them. The two appendices begin on the next page for you.

What it Means to be a Submissive Wife

∾

ULTIMATELY, WHEN A WIFE submits to her husband, she is doing it out of obedience to God. Jesus (who is co-equal to and co-eternal with God the Father and the Holy Spirit) modeled submission to us by perfectly doing the will of God the Father in everything He said and did on earth. A wife should follow this example by worshipfully surrendering her life to Christ by:

- Following her husband's leadership
- Respecting and trusting her husband's opinion
- Seeking her husband's counsel when making decisions
- Believing in her husband's ability to succeed in his areas of responsibility
- Being her husband's helpmate
- Honoring her husband by talking about him in a positive way
- Praising, affirming, and appreciating her husband
- Being a team player
- Being her husband's #1 fan!
- Serving her husband with sacrificial love
- Avoiding non-biblical criticism or nagging
- Not comparing him unfavorably to others
- Not blaming or controlling him
- Not correcting him in front of others

A wife will ultimately answer to God for how well she submits to her husband's leadership whether or not he is making good, loving decisions. However, a wife should not follow her husband into sinful behavior, for God is her ultimate authority.

When a wife is not happy with the direction her husband is leading she should take her frustrations to God with an open teachable spirit. God may be doing a work inside of her through her obedience to submit. God may be protecting her through the direction her husband is leading over what she feels is best. God may want her to lovingly share her thoughts with her husband on why they should follow a different path. God may want to work on her husband's heart while she submits her desires to the Lord. God does not need her to be the Holy Spirit, or a "holy nag." God wants her to trust Him to meet her needs and give her the proper response.

God ultimately wants you to operate together as one with your husband. Pray for God to either change your husband's mind or change your heart. In doing this, instead of requiring perfect behavior from two imperfect people, you are looking for the perfect protection and guidance from our perfect God.

APPENDIX 2

What it Means to be a Godly Husband

છ્ય

- **Individual scheduled prayer.** I (Ed) pray each morning in the shower. I pick shower time because it is something I do every day. It does not matter when you pray; it only matters that you are consistent with it.
- **Individual random prayer.** Pray for the events of the day. For example, I often pray before meetings, mentoring sessions, and time with friends or family. Angie and I often silently pray for our couples during our mentoring sessions.
- **Couple/family scheduled prayer.** Have a set time at least once a week for a prayer session. Angie and I meet twenty minutes before we would normally leave for church each week to pray as a couple. Many couples pray together more often. Some couples pray in bed together every day. Praying with and for your wife at the end of the day can be some of the best foreplay.
- **Couple/family random prayer.** Pray as a couple for special events and situations. Remember, prayer can be anywhere even in a car or an elevator.
- **Attend church.** Many Christians will attend church when it is convenient. Make attending church as a family a priority.
- **Spend time in God's word.** This is a way God can talk to us, and a relationship requires two-way communication. The more of the Bible we comprehend, the better we are prepared to deal with the world.
- **Give your time, talents, and treasures to God.** A great way to give your time and talents is to get involved in a ministry. When Angie and I got involved in the premarital counseling program at church, we did it to give back to God. Little did we know that God was going to pour out blessing on us. Remember, your first ministry is to your wife and kids. In Malachi 3:10 God ask us to test Him in our giving. He promises to open the floodgates of heaven and pour out so much blessing that there will not be room enough to store it.

- **Make godly decisions.** Big decisions require God at the center. Pray about it, see what the Bible has to say about it, listen carefully to what your wife has to say about it, seek the counsel of Christian mentors, and then make your decision.

- **Love your wife selflessly.** Husbands are instructed to sacrificially love their wives using Jesus as their example. This means doing what is most loving even if it is not what is easiest or what you want for yourself.

  > Husbands, love your wives, just as Christ loved the church and gave himself up for her.... In this same way, husbands ought to love their wives as their own bodies. He who loves his wife loves himself. After all, no one ever hated his own body, but he feeds and cares for it, just as Christ does the church—for we are members of his body.
  >
  > —Ephesians 5:25, 28-30

- **Love God.** God's greatest commandment is to love God with all your heart, soul, mind, and strength.

  Love others. God's second greatest commandment is to love others.

3. **Describe the kind of prayer life you want to have together when you get married.**

Ideally you should pray these four ways:

- Individually at set times
- Individually spontaneously
- Together at set times
- Together spontaneously

If you are not comfortable praying together, perhaps you could start by committing to pray together for a few minutes every week before you go to church. Try to incorporate these elements into your prayer: praising, asking, repenting, and thanksgiving.

Most people view sex as the most intimate interaction between a husband and wife, but truly, prayer is the most intimate communion. In sex you bare your body, but in prayer you bare your soul. It doesn't get more personal than that!

Prayer is the most important component to ensure that your love will last a lifetime.

4. **How can your fiancé be praying for you right now?**

Regularly asking your partner how you can pray for him or her is a great habit. Sometimes people have a hard time asking for prayer. If you are truly to come together as one, then you need to share your heart's desires with your future spouse. This is important to the intimacy of your relationship.

5. **How often do you read the Bible?**

You have probably heard the quote: "The truth shall set you free." This verse is not complete without the prior statement. "If you hold to my teaching, you are really my disciples. Then you will know the truth, and the truth will set you free" (John 8:31-32). We cannot know God's freedom and His will without understanding and obeying His teaching.

6. **What sin in your life right now is keeping you from being closer to God?**

    Many Christians have a "sin of choice" that they are able to justify. They live a "mostly" sin-free life except for the one sin for which they are willing to give themselves a mulligan. If we want God's best, we need to confess our sin and be willing to turn away from it.

    Counselor note: Ask their fiancé if this is how they would answer the question for their partner. Is there anything more that they would identify?

7. **What are ten things in your life for which you are thankful?**

    An attitude of gratitude is one of the most important elements for growing in our faith and our personal relationship with the Lord. The secret to joy is to see God in all our circumstances. God wants us to see His goodness in the midst of our happy times and our troubles

8. **If you and your fiancé have a major decision, what process would you use to ensure you will make a God-honoring decision?**

    If you have a clear-cut process for making big decisions, you will be able to more naturally default to it in times of stress. It should include:

    - praying to understand God's will
    - reading the Bible to get direction
    - discussing it thoroughly as a couple
    - seeking the advice of Christians you respect

    Remember, God should be the pilot, not the co-pilot, when making a decision.

    - Do you have any questions on chapter four?

CHAPTER 5

Developing an Intentional Marriage

1. **Dr. Willard F. Harley Jr. identified the following ten needs in his book, *His Needs, Her Needs*. Number in order of importance the five that you believe will be most important to you in marriage.**

Order of Top Five Needs	Need
	Admiration
	Affection
	Sexual fulfillment
	Conversation
	Family commitment
	Financial security
	Honesty and openness
	Help around the house
	Recreational companionship
	Attractive partner

2. **How can your fiancé be intentional about meeting the needs you outlined above?**

   Some desires you may have are: a weekly date night; time to talk about light topics; fun together doing a hobby; cuddle time; transparency with the finances; home cooked meals; staying physically fit; entertaining with family and friends; hearing affirming statements; having intimate, open, honest conversations; etc.

3. **When your partner doesn't meet your expectations and needs, how should you respond?**

   There will be times when you should share your unmet expectations and needs with your fiancé so that he or she can be better about meeting them. There will be other times in your relationship when it will be more profitable to take the focus off of your partner meeting your needs and put it onto God. Philippians 4:19 assures us, "God will meet all your needs according to his glorious riches in Christ Jesus." Remember that God promises to meet our needs, not our greed. This concept is explained with excellent clarity in the book, *Love Focused*, by Bob and Judy Hughes.

4. **List at least five intentional things you can do to keep your relationship strong.**

   The best way to approach having an intentional marriage is to always be thinking of things you can do to improve your relationship without expecting anything in return.

5. **On a scale of 1 to 10, ten being the most, how responsible is your fiancé for your happiness?**

6. **How good is your partner about making you happy today?**

   A key factor to happiness in life is to lower the expectations we have of others. Having high expectations of others will lead to a frustrated life of unmet expectations.

As you enter marriage, if you increase what you do for your partner and take the focus off of what you expect from him or her, you will be much happier in your marriage.

We should not hold our fiancé or anyone else responsible for making us happy. Our joy should be found solely in the Lord. God promises that as we follow His commands, we will be filled with his joy. "These things I have spoken to you, that my joy may be in you, and that your joy may be full" (John 15:11).

7. **If one day your fiancé said, "You are going to be king/queen for the day. Give me a list of five special things I can do for you today," what items would you list? What day of the week would you like to be your king/queen day?**

This is a fun exercise we highly encourage you to incorporate into your relationship each week. Even if your relationship gets a little off track, you know there are two days in the week that will help you reset and get back on track.

You may ask your fiancé to give you a foot massage, go with you to a favorite restaurant, take a walk with you, read the Bible with you, wash the car, or go with you to the movies. Be creative—the sky is the limit!

• Do you have any questions on chapter five?

CHAPTER 6

Finding the Sweet Spot in your Relationship

1. How would you define the sweet spot in your relationship, and when do you know you are in it?

The sweet spot is when you and your fiancé feel connected in all areas—emotional, physical, spiritual, and social. Everything is flowing in a positive way. Interaction is pleasant, happy, kind, and loving. There is harmony in the relationship and you are feeling oneness.

The opposite of the sweet spot is the sour patch. When you are not connecting emotionally, physically, spiritually, and socially you have drifted into the sour patch. When you are in the sour patch you are no longer experiencing oneness. Satan's favorite attack on marriage is to destroy oneness.

When you are in your sweet spot, you take things the right way. Conversely, when you are in the sour patch, you often take things wrong and even small disagreements get blown out of proportion.

Dwelling in the sweet spot in your relationship will draw you together in a lasting and intimate way that grows stronger every year. In this way, you can experience the promise of two becoming one, as expressed in Genesis 2:24. You will experience the joy and contentment that God has planned for you in marriage.

2. **You will be asked by your counselors to give a recap of the tools outlined in this chapter. Which tools mentioned are you most likely to use?**

Mentor note: The couples have been asked to review the tools that begin on the next page and to come prepared to share their understanding about them. Ask your couple to close their books. Have the woman explain the odd numbered skills and the man explain the even numbered skills. Make sure they both have a clear understanding of all of them.

TOOLS FOR STAYING IN THE SWEET SPOT

1. **Prayer.** When a couple has drifted into the sour patch and humbly comes before God together in prayer, they are more receptive to setting aside their individual agendas and selfish desires, and are open to seeking the will of God who loves them and wants them to operate as one. Imagine how useful it would be to pray as a couple when things start to enter the sour patch. This should always be a tool for the man to consider as the spiritual leader of the family, although a woman can always suggest praying together too.

2. **"I'm sorry. I win!"** Use this tactic to take advantage of your competitive nature and make a game out of forgiving quickly. Whoever says they are sorry first, wins! Now instead of letting little things fester, if one of you will quickly say sorry (knowing they just won), you can move forward with a smile. It's a great way to solve a problem and win at the same time. Angie and I (Ed) had cross words one day just as I was getting ready to leave for a meeting. Just after I left the house, I received a text from Angie that read, "I'm sorry." A few seconds later I received a second text that read, "I win!" It made me laugh and we were quickly back in our sweet spot.

3. **Fun.** For the health of your relationship, it is important to keep fun alive, but this is an area that will disappear when you are in the sour patch. Even if you are not feeling it, plan something fun that you both will enjoy doing together. The simpler the better. Some couples like going back to doing something they enjoyed when they were first dating. Couples should be able to bring out the playful child in each other. Laughter should flow freely. It has been said that fun is the litmus test for a good relationship. Good marriages have fun, and marriages that have fun are good.

4. **Mad for five minutes.** There are times that you would like to let your fiancé know that you are a little upset, but you don't want to make a mountain out of a molehill. An effective way to communicate your displeasure to your fiancé and still keep things in perspective is to say, "I am going to be mad at you for

five minutes." You both may laugh at the comment, but the point will have been made.

5. **Act of kindness.** Doing a loving act of kindness towards your fiancé when you are not feeling it is a great way to let your partner know how committed you are to getting back into the sweet spot.

6. **Love graffiti on the mirror.** Use a dry erase marker to write a love note to your fiancé. Keep an assortment of dry erase markers in your bathroom so you can be creative with your notes.

7. **"How full is your love tank?"** Ask your fiancé, "On a scale of one to ten, how full is your love tank right now?" Follow up by asking, "What would it take to make it a ten?" (This one is especially good for us guys because it comes with instructions).

8. **Replace a criticism with an affirmation.** When you are tempted to criticize your fiancé, stop yourself and instead replace the critique with a genuine affirmation. Criticism is one of the quickest ways to drive your relationship into the sour patch. By giving an affirmation, instead of making the situation worse, you make it better.

9. **Smile.** A simple smile can change the entire chemistry between you and your partner. A smile will warm the heart of your fiancé. A smile makes you appear more attractive. Studies have shown that smiling reduces blood pressure, lowers stress, boosts your immune system, releases endorphins, makes you more positive, and builds confidence. Smiles are contagious, so be the initiator.

10. **Ten things I love about you.** In your first session you each made a list of "Ten Things I Love About You." When you are drifting into the sour patch, pull these lists out and re-read what you love about your spouse and what they love about you. Once your heart is softened, ask your fiancé to do the same. Now, each of you should add one more new thing to your list.

11. **Big picture.** When you and your fiancé have an argument, ask yourself, "In the scope of eternity, does this really matter? For the sake of our relationship, can I just let it go?"

12. **Text.** Sometimes a loving text is all it takes to get back into the sweet spot. Recently Angie's phone was nearing the memory limit and she asked me to help her free some memory. I asked her if I could delete her text messages for the last two years. She said, "Yes, all except yours." She explained that occasionally she likes to go back and reread my loving text messages.

13. **King/queen for the day.** You learned this in an earlier chapter. Hopefully this is something you will incorporate into your weekly calendar. This is a relationship game-changer. It brings your relationship into the sweet spot at least two days per week.

14. **Special time.** Special time is one-to-one connected time together. It is important to keep dating even after you get married. It doesn't have to be fancy or expensive. It just needs to be kept a priority.

15. **"I love you."** These words can be music to your partner's ears. Add a hug and a long romantic kiss for extra credit.

16. **Start all over.** Occasionally you have a day that seems to go sideways from the start. When this happens, all it takes is for one of you to say, "Can we start over?" By prior mutual agreement, this is a pact to start over with no talk of what may have caused the day to go wrong in the first place. This cannot be used for major problems, but is an excellent tool for small problems.

17. **Love and respect.** Women want to be cherished by their husbands and men want to be respected by their wives. When you are married, continually do things to make your wife feel special and adored by you (especially in front of others). Let her know you are her protector and will keep her safe and secure. As a wife, continually show your husband you are on his team and his biggest fan. Believe in him and avoid questioning or challenging him in front of others.

18. **Make it between you and God.** Make it between you and God instead of you and your spouse. Do the right thing because you want to be pleasing to God, even if you are not feeling it towards your fiancé in that moment.

A relationship never stays the same: it either gets better or bitter. The words *better* and *bitter* differ only in whether the first vowel is an "e" or an "i." An easy way to remember how a relationship becomes bitter is by emphasizing that the "i" in *bitter* indicates a self-centered relationship. An easy way to remember how to make your relationship better is by emphasizing the "e" in *better* is for Emmanuel. *Emmanuel* means "God is with us." To sum up, a Christ-centered (better) marriage is a life-long commitment that requires a vital connection with Christ.

The stresses of life may challenge or even discourage you at times, but there is no reason for your relationship to drift into the sour patch for very long. Be committed to using some of the skills outlined here and developing some of your own to quickly get back into the sweet spot.

A great thought to remember is, *I have suffered a great many catastrophes in my life, most of which never happened.*

3. **Share a memory of the two of you having fun together.**

Fun is the litmus test of a good marriage. If you are having fun together, your relationship is doing well. Conversely, if your relationship is not doing well, you will find that you are no longer having fun together. As you recall your favorite memories together, you may notice that these moments did not necessarily cost a lot of money. Usually they are more about the connectedness you are feeling with each other at the time. You are in the sweet spot!

If you are ever struggling with having fun together, try watching blooper videos of your favorite sitcoms. You will end up laughing together and laughter is such a bonding and healing gift.

• Do you have any question on chapter six?

Closing Comments

- Set up time for your next session.

- Ask your couple to pray together during the next week.

- Close in prayer.

Session III

Before You Meet

Depending on your couple's spiritual maturity, you may want to ask one (or both) to close your session in prayer. If you detect they may be hesitant or embarrassed, then you or your spouse should take the lead.

Here are some additional tips:

o One of the great values of mentoring couple-to-couple is that men and women sense things differently. If you intuitively sense there is more to someone's answer than what they've spoken, try to draw out their feelings by saying, "Tell me more," or asking open-ended questions such as, "I sense there is a little more that you have to say on this. Will you elaborate?" This is especially important on topics that are difficult for them to discuss. You can also use statements like, "What do you think about what your partner just shared?" or "Explain a little more about what you are trying to say."

o If you can see areas of growth that need a little extra work, don't hesitate to give them extra homework assignments that help them grow in these areas. Examples might be to pray together as a couple, encourage each other throughout the week in a challenging area, or find a new way to speak in each other's love language.

o Each week it is important that you read the mentor's notes for each of the three chapters so you understand each question's purpose in the chapter. In addition, it is essential for you to be familiar with the chapter content in the couple's workbook for the three chapters you will be covering during the session.

CHAPTER 7

Personality Differences

- Ask your couple if they have been faithful to their premarital covenant.

- Ask your couple if they prayed together this week.

- Ask your couple if they completed the King/Queen for the day assignment this week.

1. **Do you believe you and your fiancé are compatible? Explain.**

   A great marriage is not based on marrying someone compatible because God does not make any two people perfectly compatible; it is based on learning how to deal effectively with your incompatibilities.

2. **The statements below reflect personality traits. On a scale of 1 to 10, describe how well the statement applies to you.**

   1 = does not describe at all
   10 = very accurately describes me

   As your couple rates themselves on the statements below, watch for big differences and have them discuss those differences. Remind them these are just possible differences. There is not a right or wrong to them.

	Statement	Rating (1–10)
A	I prefer to think things through carefully before moving in new directions.	
B	I enjoy being recognized publicly for my achievements.	
C	I generally don't like change.	
D	I have a daily to-do list and try to complete it.	
E	I am very spontaneous.	
F	I am very neat and tidy. I like things in their place.	
G	I am rarely late to an appointment, meeting, or event.	
H	I feel a sense of accomplishment when I complete a project. I am reluctant to start new projects until I finish the one I am working on.	
I	I prefer socializing in small groups (ideally with just one other couple), rather than at big parties.	

- Do you have any questions on chapter seven?

CHAPTER 8

Differences between Men and Women

1. How do you believe the general differences between men and women will affect your decision-making process in marriage?

You should recognize the unique point of view that each of you can bring to the discussion. Because women use both sides of their brain simultaneously, they usually weigh the emotional ramifications involved in any decision. They tend to be more relational, sensitive, intuitive, and compassionate. A woman should be aware that she needs to look at some decisions more logically and suppress the emotional side; conversely, a man should value the emotional aspects that his wife brings into some decisions that he looks at purely logically.

Men tend to operate more dominantly out of one side of the brain or the other. When a man becomes very emotional, he may no longer view things in his common logical manner. When this occurs, it is best if a wife does not push to resolve the issue right then. If you try to present the logical way to view things at this time, it will likely escalate emotions. Let some time elapse and then revisit the issue. When you understand these differences, you will be able to appreciate how men and women complement each other and can work together to make better decisions.

2. **Men and women get their self-esteem in different ways. Taking this into consideration, how could you help strengthen your partner's self-esteem?**

To the woman: A man generally gets his self-esteem from his career and by providing for his family. You should be sensitive to this by believing in your man, being interested in his career, appreciating his efforts, and respecting him, especially in public. In short, you need to be your man's **number one fan!**

To the man: In general, a woman gets her self-esteem from her relationships. The most important relationship is you. You should be sensitive to this important role in your fiancée's life, and affirm her, appreciate her, and build her up daily. Let her know you want to protect her and keep her safe. Communicate to her how **special she is to you** and that you cherish her!

Everyone should ultimately receive his or her self-esteem from God. A strong sense of who we are in Christ minimizes our need to draw on our partner so heavily to build up our self-esteem.

3. **Men and women have different conversational needs. Has this created a problem in your relationship? If so, how? What solutions do you suggest?**

You likely have different needs for sharing so it is important for each of you to be sensitive to the other. Women tend to give more detail when talking, which can frustrate a man. Women can feel as though their thoughts and ideas are being dismissed, thus making them feel devalued in the eyes of their partner. Women should be sensitive to this and try to bottom-line their conversation, while men should be sensitive to truly listening and validating their mate's input.

You should make a priority of having time together each day to communicate. You may need some down time when you first arrive home from work before diving into big conversation. It is also best to avoid talking about heavy issues when you are hungry or tired. Ultimately, there should be some prime time that is reserved each day for you to come together in meaningful conversation.

Although both men and women benefit by having same-sex friendships, it especially helps women, who typically have greater relational needs. A wife should seek out God-honoring relationships with other women. But don't use these relationships as a place to complain about your husband, but rather to learn to be a better wife (and, perhaps down the road, a better mother too).

4. **Although men and women do not think alike, being able to see things from your partner's perspective will help strengthen your relationship and create better teamwork. What are some creative ways you can suggest for learning and understanding what is important to your fiancé?**

First and foremost, ask your partner to share what is important to him or her. When you do this, reflective listening is a great tool to make sure you are grasping what they are sharing. After your fiancé shares his or her thoughts, reflective listening involves you restating what you understood him or her to say so he or she can clarify any misunderstanding.

A second way to insure that your partner comprehends what you are trying to communicate is to use a word picture that is relatable to him or her so that he or she can emotionally connect.

• Do you have any questions on chapter eight?

CHAPTER 9

Love Languages

- Please share the results of "The Five Love Languages" tests, which can be found in your workbook in appendix 3 for women and appendix 4 for men.

- If you look at the "Love Languages Guide" in appendix 5 in your workbook, you will see basic actions to take and avoid for each love language.

Mentor note: Appendix 5 from the workbook appears on the next page.

Love Languages Guide

ひ

Love Language	Actions	Avoid
Words of Affirmation	• Compliments • Notes and cards • Kind words	Criticism
Quality Time	• One-to-one time • Face-to-face interaction • Taking long walks together • Doing activities together	Allowing other people or priorities to interrupt special time together
Receiving Gifts	• Giving gifts on special and not-so-special days • More about the thoughtfulness of the gift than the expense of the gift	Ignoring or forgetting special days
Acts of Service	• Helping with chores • Saying things like, "How can I help you?"	Helping others and not being there for your spouse
Physical Touch	• Touches • Hugs & cuddling • Kisses	Negative touch

Chart based on Gary Chapman's book, *The Five Love Languages*.

When you understand the concept of speaking in the five different love languages, you will be able to enhance all of your relationships. You can learn the love languages of those closest to you and relate to them in the way that is most meaningful to them. You can access the love language assessment for free on-line.

1. On a scale of 1 to 10, how full is your love tank?

2. What could your fiancé do to raise it to a 10?

3. Complete this sentence, "I feel most loved when …"

Use the three questions above to occasionally take inventory of how well you are meeting each other's needs and to know how you can better meet those needs.

- Any questions on chapter nine?

Closing Comments

- Next week we will discuss families so please bring some pictures of your families. Pictures on your phone are fine.

- Set up time for your next session.

- Close in prayer.

Session IV

Before You Meet

This is perhaps one of the most important sessions you will have with your couple. If this session is successful, your couple will be able to establish a meaningful connection and appropriate boundaries with their extended family, will gain new communication skills, and will be equipped with a method to assist them in resolving their conflicts. Wow—what a difference you will be making in their lives!

Here are some additional tips:

o   Most sessions are designed to last about an hour and a half. This session may last longer so pace yourself and focus on what is most important. Quickly move to the next question if you can see that your couple is strong in that area.

o   Be aware of what your couple is saying during your session, not only through words, but also through body language. By now they should be placing Christ at the center of their relationship and should be creating a practice of praying together. If they are not doing so, then nicely, but firmly, hold them accountable. The husband should hold the man accountable and the wife should hold the woman accountable.

o   The "Ten Steps to Resolve Conflict" your couple will be introduced to in this session will be a valuable tool for their relationship. Ask your couple to view the online video dramatization of a couple working through a conflict that is located on the website at http://marriagebygod.org. If they have an actual conflict to work through, ask them to do it as an extra homework assignment and share the results with you when you meet for your next session.

o   Each week it is important that you read the mentor's notes for each of the three chapters so you understand each question's purpose in the chapter. In addition, it is essential for you to be familiar with the chapter content in the couple's workbook for the three chapters you will be covering during the session.

CHAPTER 10

Extended Family

- Ask your couple if they have been faithful to their premarital covenant.

- Ask your couple if they prayed together this past week.

- Ask your couple if they completed the King/Queen for the day assignment this past week.

- Did you bring a picture of your family to share?

Do you know why we wear our wedding rings on our fourth finger? Let me share a little illustration with you. Bring your two open hands together. Now, bend your middle fingers at the knuckle and bring them together. Have your remaining fingers all touch tip to tip. As you observe your hands in this manner your middle fingers represent God at the center of your marriage relationship. Your thumbs represent your parents. Try to pull your thumbs apart. They come apart very easily. This is because we are meant to grow up and leave our parents' household. Our pointer fingers represent our siblings. These fingers also separate easily because our siblings also grow up and leave their parents' house. Our little fingers represent our children. Once again, these fingers separate because our children too are meant to grow up and leave their parents' household. However, when you hold your fingertips together and try to separate your ring fingers, you cannot do it. This is because God intends for marriage to last a lifetime. What God joins together, let no one separate.

1. **What does Genesis 2:24, "Therefore a man shall leave his father and mother and be joined to his wife, and they shall become one flesh," mean to you?**

   As you come together in marriage, the two of you become your own primary family unit. You should still show love and respect to your extended family, but you have the highest loyalty and devotion to one another.

2. **Describe the relationship you have with your parents. How has this relationship shaped or impacted your view of marriage?**

   Whether we like it or not, our relationship with our parents and what was modeled to us growing up impacts our own relationship with our spouse. We either live what we learned (sometimes without realizing it) or intentionally choose to live differently. Sometimes we transfer emotional needs that were not appropriately met by our parents into our marriage in an unhealthy way. Acknowledging how these parts of our history play into our marriage leads to new healthier patterns.

3. **Do you ever share relationship problems with a family member?**

   Vigilantly resist sharing marital problems with parents or siblings. This is tempting when you are frustrated or hurting. The problem is that after you resolve the conflict, your family will still remember the hurt your spouse caused you even after you've long forgotten it. These situations can cause great misunderstanding and can drive a wedge into family relationships that can be difficult to remove.

4. **On a scale of 1 to 10 (10 being best), how would you rate your relationship with your future in-laws? Explain.**

If you rate the relationship as a 10, there is only one direction for it to go. Give the relationship room and time to grow. If you rate the relationship low, remember that negative talk about your in-laws can still be very hurtful to your fiancé (even if it is true). When relationships get off to a challenging beginning, they can still get better over time if you continue to respond in love. Don't be controlled by their response, but love them where they are because that is what God calls you to do.

A good thing to remember is that your own parents will be much more understanding of you than of your spouse. If you have negative news to deliver to your parents, such as, "We will not be able to attend a family event with you because we have another commitment," you should each make sure that you deliver the news to your own parents. Conversely, whenever you have an opportunity to deliver good news try to be the one to tell your in-laws. This will help create a positive relationship with the in-laws.

5. **What issues with your extended family may create a strain on your marriage?**

Extended family can be a source of friction between couples. The most important objective when dealing with family is that you and your fiancé maintain a united front. Discuss problems together. Show compassion for your partner's struggles. Pray together for a good resolution. Draw on the strength of the Holy Spirit to give you a united attitude toward your family, and then family challenges will not tear you apart, but will strengthen you.

6. **Describe in detail where and with whom you will spend your first Thanksgiving and Christmas.**

You may not be able to spend equal time with both families each year. If this is sensitive, look to make it as fair as you can over the years.

7. **What can you do to express your love to your parents and future in-laws?**

You might want to write them a note or take them out with the specific intention of expressing that you are looking forward to having them as in-laws and that you are thankful to them for giving you such a wonderful fiancé. You could also write a note to your parents and give it to them right before the wedding, thanking them and telling them how much you love them. One more thing you can do for your parents and in-laws is to always keep them in your prayers.

• Any questions on chapter ten?

CHAPTER 11

Communication

1. **Which of the communication styles below describe your fiancé? Check all that apply.**

   ☐ **Communicates with lack of detail.**

   ☐ **Communicates with excessive detail.**

   ☐ **Communicates with a loud or angry voice.**

   ☐ **Fails to communicate things that I should know; for example, does not tell me about an upcoming social engagement until days after he or she knew about it.**

   ☐ **Often does not communicate what he or she is really thinking.**

   ☐ **Often becomes defensive when discussing things.**

   ☐ **Communicates things that are intentionally hurtful.**

   ☐ **Retreats and stops communicating at all.**

   ☐ **Other_____.**

   Do you agree with the observations your partner made about areas of communication that need some growth in your relationship? The first step towards correcting a problem is acknowledging the role you play in it. Once the communication shortcoming is identified, you can agree as a couple to nicely point out when your partner slips into a negative communication pattern. Agree in advance that when your partner does this, you will attempt to correct the problem without being defensive so you can work towards building healthier communication habits.

2. **On a scale of 1 to 10, ten being best, how would you rate your partner's listening skills?**

Few skills are more important in a marriage than listening. Skilled listeners focus on what is being said rather than thinking about how they are going to respond to what is being said. Reflective listening (asking your partner to repeat back what they just heard you say) is a good way to make sure that you are being understood.

Sometimes, it isn't so much that you aren't being heard, but that you aren't being understood. One way to enable your words to penetrate your partner's heart so that they truly understand and feel your words' impact is to use emotional word pictures. To learn more about this communication tool, read *The Language of Love* by Gary Smalley and John Trent.

3. **Does your fiancé interrupt you? If yes, how does it make you feel?**

Some women converse in an interactive listening style that can be interpreted as interrupting, but this is not meant to be disrespectful. If this is an issue in your communication, the woman should understand that her guy might be frustrated by it. A man should understand that this is not meant to be disrespectful. Be patient and understanding with one another. This typically only becomes a problem when you are not dwelling in your sweet spot. Try to resolve the core problem that has pulled you into the sour patch.

4. **How often does your fiancé criticize you?**

Excessive criticism is one of the most common destroyers of relationships. Most of us are aware of how often we are criticized, but we are seldom aware of how often we criticize.

A good rule is not to criticize your fiancé more than once per week. If you criticize your partner on Monday, you are done for the week. When you are tempted to criticize, affirm instead and you will soon see a big change in your relationship.

When you receive a criticism, there are three basic ways in which you can receive it.

  a) You can deeply resent the criticism. This allows your hurt to turn to poison in your heart, which ultimately hurts you, not the other person.

  b) You can lash out towards your partner. This just escalates things in a negative direction. If you are right, no defense is necessary. If you are wrong, no defense will do.

  c) You can receive the lesson and release the lesion. Although a criticism by nature may sting, there can be an element of truth to what is being said. Evaluate the criticism to receive any constructive criticism and release any hurt to God.

Many proverbs address the fact that the wise welcome criticism, rebuke, and reproof, but fools hate and reject it. If you have trouble with criticism, a good homework assignment would be to read a chapter of Proverbs a day for a month, matching the chapter number to the day of the month. Remember that God is love, love is kind, and God rebukes, so not all rebukes are unkind.

5. Give an example of when your fiancé was brutally honest instead of lovingly honest with you. How could he or she have communicated better in that situation?

When you are lovingly honest, you are delivering honesty in a loving way. When you are brutally honest, you are delivering honesty in a way that is meant to hurt.

Before you speak, ask yourself if what you are about to say is kind, necessary, and true. If you cannot answer yes to all three, then hold your thought.

If you are anxious to confront a situation and are not able to do it in a kind way, then perhaps it is not the right time. Allow yourself time to gather your thoughts so you can speak truth with love and kindness. Brutal honesty is never appropriate.

6. **When you are in the sweet spot in your relationship, do you still experience communication problems?**

Couples who are experiencing difficulty in their relationship often express that they are having communication problems. The truth is that faulty communication is usually not the problem, but a symptom of a problem or problems. However, improving your communication skills can often be the first step towards addressing the real issue. In the next chapter, we are going to learn ways to resolve the core problem.

• Do you have any questions on chapter eleven?

CHAPTER 12

Resolving Conflict

1. What is the difference between a discussion and an argument?

In an argument, the parties try to prove *who* is right, whereas in a discussion, they try to determine *what* is right. In an argument there is competition. In a discussion there is collaboration.

A sure way to turn a discussion into an argument is to criticize or attack personally. The best ways to turn an argument into a discussion are to begin acknowledging areas where you agree with the other person so you can begin collaborating, or to set a time in the future to discuss the problem so that emotions can cool down. The keys are to avoid escalating discussions into arguments and to calm arguments into discussions.

Refer to appendix 6 in your workbook to review the "Rules for Discussion." Having sound rules for discussions will help minimize arguments.

Mentor note: Appendix 6 from the workbook appears on the next page.

Appendix 6

Rules for Discussion

❧

1. Speak in a quiet voice.
2. Do not interrupt.
3. Do not bring up the past.
4. Do not blame.
5. Do not use profanity.
6. Do not criticize.
7. Use "I feel" statements, not attacking "you" statements.
8. State *your* feelings, not your partner's.
9. Never threaten your relationship.

Any questions on the Rules for Discussion? Work on incorporating these rules into your everyday conversations.

2. **Name one or more minor conflicts in your relationship that do not need to be resolved (a minor conflict is a conflict that does not cause harm to the relationship, or a conflict that will go away on its own).**

Small conflicts do not need to be formally resolved. Anything that does not continue to drive a wedge into your relationship is a small conflict. Minor conflicts can usually be settled through compromising. For instance, suppose you want to go out to dinner, but disagree on where to go. One of you might pick three possibilities from which the other chooses. Or you might alternate who picks each time.

3. **List one or more moderate conflicts in your relationship (a moderate conflict is a conflict that does not threaten a healthy relationship, but its resolution would generate more harmony).**

An excellent tool to resolve a moderate conflict is to use the practice of *Start or Stop, and Continue.* The partner who is bothered starts by wisely choosing a time when they are both rested and can peacefully discuss the issue. Then this person lovingly explains the problem and asks the other person to either start a desired action or stop the unwanted action. He or she follows up by sharing something good they would like the partner to continue doing. Basically the hurt partner is giving a constructive criticism in a loving way, at the right time, followed by a nice affirmation. This is a sure way to resolve a moderate conflict. Remember to follow the "Rules for Discussions" discussed in appendix 6.

4. **List one or more major conflicts in your relationship (a major conflict is a significant issue that if left unresolved would damage or threaten a healthy**

relationship; or a recurring conflict that continually causes dissension).

Refer to appendix 7 in your workbook, "Ten Rules to Resolve Conflict." This is a time-tested, highly effective method for resolving conflict in a relationship. Let's take a close look at the "Ten Rules to Resolve Conflict."

Mentor note: Appendix 7 from the workbook appears on the next page.

Ten Rules to Resolve Conflict

ℰℐ

1. Define the issue to be resolved.
2. Set a time to meet.
3. Set a private place to meet.
4. Begin in prayer.
5. Each share your position.
6. Each point out what he or she has done to contribute to the problem.
7. Each point out what he or she can do to help resolve the issue.
8. Agree on a resolution acceptable to both.
9. Write down the resolution.
10. End in prayer.

Here are a few final pointers before resolving a conflict:

- Be sure to set the conflict resolution for a later time. This allows emotions to settle and provides an opportunity for both of you to think about what you want to say.
- Each of you should open in prayer. If you are uncomfortable with prayer, the prayer can be as simple as, "Please, God, be with us."
- Face each other and hold hands.
- Be sure to both complete each step before going on to the next one.
- Remember to refer to the "Ten Rules to Resolve Conflict" as often as you need to so that you don't accidentally skip a step.
- When you agree on the actions you will take to achieve your resolution, write them down and put them in a prominent place. Refer to them daily so that you stay focused and committed to your resolution.

- Do you have any questions on chapter twelve?

Closing Comments

- Set up a time for your next session.

- As additional homework, please have your couple go to the www.marriagebygod.org and watch the *Conflict Resolution Video* before the next session.

If your couple cited a major conflict when answering question 4, request that they set up time before the next session to follow the model in appendix 7, "Ten Rules to Resolve Conflict," and to come prepared to share the results at their next session.

- Close in prayer.

Session V

Before You Meet

Most likely by now your couple will be very comfortable sharing with you. Even so, your couple may be reluctant to share their deepest thoughts on emotional intimacy, especially the couples who need this chapter the most.

Here are some additional tips:

o   If you suspect your couple is avoiding sharing at a deep level, give them additional time to answer. Don't be afraid to allow for times of silence. You can also ask follow-up questions to help them open up. Remember, the success of the mentoring is based on their willingness to communicate openly and honestly with each other.

o   Sometimes couples want to compromise on some of the affair-proofing principles presented in this session. Don't let your couple compromise when it comes to understanding these concepts.

o   Each week it is important that you read the mentor's notes for each of the three chapters so you understand each question's purpose in the chapter. In addition, it is essential for you to be familiar with the chapter content in the couple's workbook for the three chapters you will be covering during the session.

CHAPTER 13

Emotional Intimacy

- Ask your couple how they did with resolving their conflict.

- Ask your couple if they prayed together this week.

- Ask your couple if they completed the King/Queen for the day again this week.

- Ask your couple if they have been faithful to their premarital covenant.

1. **On a scale of 1 to 10 (10 being best), rate the accuracy of the following statements.**

Statement	Rating
I feel emotionally connected and understood by my fiancé. If you do not feel connected, what would make you feel connected?	
I feel comfortable and safe sharing my deepest thoughts and feelings with my fiancé. If you're uncomfortable sharing your deepest thoughts, what do you fear?	

I trust my fiancé to keep my confidences.

> If trust is missing, what can your fiancé do to begin rebuilding trust? You need to give your partner a way to win.

I feel my fiancé knows me better than any other person.

> If you do not feel you know each other, spend some special time together sharing your dreams.

I believe we will make important decisions together as a team in marriage.

> God wants you to operate as a team—two becoming one. You cannot experience emotional intimacy if you are not a team. Two heads are always better than one.

I believe we will be good about holding each other accountable in a God-honoring way in marriage.

> If you see a correction your fiancé needs, do it privately and gently. Always affirm your belief that he or she can make the needed correction. Also, be receptive to receiving correction from your partner. Take personal responsibility for your failures. Do not defend or make excuses. Instead thank your fiancé for pointing them out.

We pray together as a couple on a regular basis.

> Praying together regularly at a deep, heartfelt level creates a spiritual bonding. What is standing in the way of this taking place?

2. **What is the biggest deterrent to being more vulnerable with your fiancé (such as fear of trusting, rejection, judgment, losing control, appearing weak, or getting a negative response)?**

   The imprint from our family of origin shapes our behaviors, beliefs, and expectations of all relationships, especially our marriages. Consider how your early experiences of care and comfort (or lack of care and comfort)—especially from your parents—have shaped your ability and your desire for connection and closeness. Hurts and traumas from our past cause fear or make it hard for us to trust others. If these hurts are impeding emotional intimacy with your fiancé, then you may need to get some additional help to heal those wounds.

3. **Do you see any negative behaviors hindering emotional intimacy in your relationship (such as avoidance, sarcasm, passive-aggressive behavior, criticism, nagging, anger, self-pity, defensiveness, or family-of-origin imprints)?**

   You must identify the problem before you can correct it. After you identify the problem, you must want to fix it, make a plan, and then follow the plan. What are some steps you can take to improve this negative behavior pattern?

4. **Complete this statement, "This is what I would like you to know about me in order to understand me better ..."**

   Part of developing a closer relationship and a better understanding of one another is to converse with open and honest communication about your personal thoughts and feelings.

   • Do you have any questions on chapter thirteen?

CHAPTER 14

Physical Intimacy

1. Are you comfortable discussing your future sexual needs in marriage with your fiancé?

Open, honest communication is the key to a vibrant sex life. You should be honest about what pleasures you. Mutually satisfying sexual intimacy requires being both selfish and unselfish. Great lovers know their own bodies and enjoy their sexual feelings, as well as know and meet the sexual needs of their partner. Remember, you are not mind readers. You need to honestly share with one another. Continue sharing because, especially for women, what feels good one time may not the next.

Don't think that sharing your needs and wants takes the romance out of the experience. On the contrary, it allows for better sexual intimacy. The goal should be to combine the best of what you both desire to create a fulfilling love life for both of you. You need to be honest and open with your spouse to experience the sexual fulfillment that God intended you to have in marriage.

2. What concerns or fears do you have concerning sex?

One concern that often comes up with this question is the woman feeling insecure about her looks, no matter how attractive she is. We are bombarded with images of perfect bodies in the media that even the models and actors being represented can't live up to after all of the airbrushing, etc. This can put a lot of pressure on us to feel like we need to look like the pictures we see in magazines, on billboards, and on television. Women, especially, no matter how beautiful they are, tend to feel insecure about their looks. Yet men are visually stimulated and enjoy seeing their wives naked. We need to keep two things in focus. First, God created us the way we are and we should accept ourselves as we are without comparing ourselves to others. Our fiancé chose us as a partner over billions of others in the world. Second, we should be good stewards of the body God has given us. We need to watch our health, diet, and exercise so that we can always present our best selves to our spouse.

3. **What from your or your partner's past may affect your intimacy?**

People generally don't feel uncomfortable about their own past, but they feel insecure about their partner's past. They fear they might be compared. If you are feeling self-conscious about past relationships, this can definitely affect your intimacy with your spouse. Share these feelings with your spouse. In talking about past relationships, avoid the details and just work through the issues. Be forgiving of each other and yourself. It is important to talk openly and honestly.

4. **How many times per week do you think you will desire sex in marriage? Your spouse-to-be?**

The desire for sexual intimacy within marriage is rarely equal. Our biological differences play into this a great deal. A husband is visual and can become very easily aroused by just seeing his wife's body. He can achieve sexual fulfillment within a few seconds of proper stimulation. A wife's hormones change throughout the month and can affect her sex drive. It takes more effort for her to attain sexual fulfillment. The type and duration of stimulation a wife needs during foreplay can vary greatly from one time to the next.

Never deprive your spouse the gift of your body in love.

5. **What are some creative ways you can keep the romance in your relationship?**

After marriage, it is important to continue to let your spouse know that he or she is still the love of your life by keeping romance alive. Wives especially delight in being sought after and made to feel special. You will feel most amorous when you feel a oneness with your spouse.

The need for romance is not always equal. Even if it is not as necessary for you, wouldn't you always appreciate the effort put into a romantic atmosphere? Wouldn't you enjoy your spouse doing fun romantic things to make the experience more special?

Remember to keep the fun in your sex life. Enjoy each other! Never lose the art of romancing your spouse and making an event out of your love-making moments.

- Do you have any questions on chapter fourteen?

CHAPTER 15

Affair Proofing Your Marriage

1. **In which of the following ways do you engage with friends or work associates of the opposite gender one-to-one without the knowledge of your fiancé? Check all that apply.**

    ☐ **Phone calls**

    ☐ **Email**

    ☐ **Texting**

    ☐ **Commenting on Facebook posts (or other social media)**

    ☐ **Private messaging through Facebook (or other social media)**

    ☐ **Coffee breaks**

    ☐ **Meals/drinks together**

    ☐ **Business meetings**

    ☐ **Social events**

    Outside of the workplace, it is never appropriate to carry on one-to-one, in-depth communications with someone of the opposite sex once you are engaged or married. You should either say no because you are engaged/married, or you should bring your partner into the conversation by cc'ing them or tagging them. Tell your partner about phone conversations that are not work related. Transparency is key.

Usually one-to-one social and work situations can be addressed by including a third person. If a work situation cannot be avoided, make sure that you meet at an appropriate setting for business; never an intimate setting. Also, take care to keep the conversation on business. Do not allow the conversation to become personal.

2. **Is there any relationship that you can identify as needing additional boundaries? What action steps would you suggest putting into place to improve your hedges?**

Sometimes your fiancé can intuitively sense when a relationship is getting too close between you and someone of the opposite sex. It may be completely innocent on your part, but the other person may not have such innocent intentions. Or what might be innocent right now has the potential to become inappropriate. Out of love and respect for your fiancé, take immediate and appropriate action to safeguard your relationship.

3. **What is your attitude towards pornography?**

Most people in this day and age (especially men) have viewed pornography at some point. Pornography precludes you from enjoying the closeness and intimacy God created for husbands and wives. Pornography is basically a virtual affair. It is like inviting a third party into your bedroom. Even when someone views pornography without the knowledge of their spouse, it will impact their intimacy, often by desensitizing you to your spouse.

Consider these two studies:

Christians aren't immune. When surveyed, 53% of men who attended Promise Keepers said they viewed pornography that week. More than 45% of Christians admit that pornography is a major problem in their home. An anonymous survey conducted recently by Pastors.com reported that 54% of pastors admitted viewing porn within the last year. In an online newsletter, 34% of female readers of *Today's Christian Woman* admitted to intentionally accessing Internet porn. One out of every six women who read *Today's Christian Woman* say they struggle with addiction to pornography (Today's Christian Woman, Fall 2003).[1]

For the surprising number of husbands who think that pornography use is "no big deal," consider this from those who work at ground-zero of divorce. During a recent meeting of divorce attorneys, 2/3 of the 350 attorneys said the Internet played a significant role in the divorces in the past year, with excessive interest in online porn contributing to more than half such cases. Pornography had an almost non-existent role in divorce just 10 or so years ago.[2]

4. **Will you agree to give total access to each other's technology activities? Will you agree to occasionally check each other's Internet history as an accountability partner?**

This is a very healthy and important safeguard to put in place within your relationship. The key here is transparency and accountability. Share your passwords with each other and keep each other accountable by occasionally checking your partner's history.

5. **Are you comfortable with the amount of time that your fiancé spends away from you? Explain.**

Sometimes couples can complacently drift into being like married singles. Wanting to spend time together is important. Make sure home is a welcoming place for both of you. Greet each other in a loving way when you come together at the end of the day. If your fiancé is engaged in hobbies or outside activities that you can participate in or support as a viewer or fan, be there. If your partner has to work long hours for a

---

[1] Paul Coughlin, "Pornography and Virtual Infidelity," *Focus on the Family*, accessed May 22, 2015,
http://www.focusonthefamily.com/marriage/divorce-and-infidelity/pornography-and-virtual-infidelity/virtual-infidelity-and-marriage.

[2] Paul Coughlin, "Erosive Influence of Port Upon Husbands," *Focus on the Family*, accessed May 22, 2015,
http://www.focusonthefamily.com/marriage/divorce-and-infidelity/pornography-and-virtual-infidelity/erosive-influence-of-porn-on-husbands.

season, meet up for a meal or surprise them by bringing them a treat.

6. List five activities or hobbies you enjoy doing together.

It is important to continue to find things you enjoy doing together. Over the years, couples often find that their interests and activities take them in different directions and they begin to grow apart. Be intentional about continuing to find new ways you enjoy spending time together.

- Do you have any questions on chapter fifteen?

At this time, the guys are going to meet separately in another room while the ladies stay here.

Mentor note: The purpose of separating is three fold.

1. Discuss something with the man or woman that you would not want to discuss as a couple.
2. Ask them if they have any questions for you that they want to ask without their partner present.
3. Review "Ten Ways to be a Fantastic Wife/Husband" in appendix 8 or 9.

Mentor note: Appendices 8 and 9 from the workbook begin on the next page.

Ten Ways to be a Fantastic Wife

❧

1. Believe in your husband and be his number one fan.
2. Be careful not to nag your husband. Turn over your concerns to God in prayer. Ask God to give you oneness in your marriage.
3. It is not uncommon for a husband to have a greater sex drive than his wife. Take care of his sexual needs.
4. On the first day of each month, put the following question on your calendar: "What must it be like to be married to me?"
5. People tend to be what you say they are. Tell your husband what a great husband, friend, and lover he is. He won't disappoint you.
6. When you come together at the end of the day, greet each other in a loving way.
7. Guys are visual; do your best to take care of yourself and be attractive to him.
8. Remember to speak in his love language.
9. Share in his hobbies with him. Continue to be the fun person he married.
10. Put Christ at the center of your life and at the center of your marriage.

APPENDIX 9

Ten Ways to be a Fantastic Husband

Ꮗ

1. Always show your wife how special she is to you.
2. Avoid being too critical. What you may think of as constructive criticism, she may see as an attack on her.
3. If you want to have a great sex life, you must keep some romance in your relationship. Continue to date your wife!
4. On the first day of each month, put the following question on your calendar: "What must it be like to be married to me?"
5. Write down your wife's anniversary, her birthday, and Valentine's Day, and put them on your calendar. Log yourself a reminder for each December 31 to add these dates to the next year's calendar.
6. Compliment your wife's appearance. She knows you are visual. Your compliments are important to her.
7. People tend to be what you say they are. Tell your wife what a great wife, friend, and lover she is. She won't disappoint you.
8. Remember to talk in her love language.
9. Your wife will need to talk. Take time to be a good listener. Often, she won't want a solution; she will just want to talk to you. Value her opinion.
10. Put Christ at the center of your life and marriage, and be the spiritual leader of your family. Ask your wife how you can be praying for her.

After reviewing the *10 Ways to be a Fantastic Wife/Husband,* the four of you should come back together to finish the session.

Closing Comments

- Set up a time for your next session.
- Close in prayer.

Session VI

Before You Meet

As mentors, be sure to finish strong. Some mentors like to finish by getting together with their couple for a meal. If you choose to do this, we recommend that you do it as a seventh meeting, not as part of this sixth session.

Here are some additional tips:

o Depending on your skill in finance, you may feel comfortable in reviewing your couple's *Budget* and *Financial Statement,* or you may elect to skip this process. At least make sure that they have completed both.

o Unless finance is one of their strengths, strongly encourage them to enroll in a Dave Ramsey or Crown Ministry Workshop. The information for both is in their workbook.

o Each week it is important that you read the mentor's notes for each of the three chapters so you understand each question's purpose in the chapter. In addition, it is essential for you to be familiar with the chapter in the couple's workbook for the three chapters you will be covering during the session.

o This is a very important week and you want to make sure that your couple has a good grasp of the concepts and skills that were introduced throughout the program.

o Write on your calendar to send your couple an encouraging note or email the week of their wedding. Continue to keep them in your prayers.

As you wrap up this final session, recognize that you have just done some incredible work for God. When one marriage improves, it can affect generations to come. May you be blessed for the blessing you have given!

CHAPTER 16

Finances

- Ask your couple if they prayed together this week.

- Ask your couple if they completed the King/Queen for the day again this week.

- Ask your couple if they have been faithful to their premarital covenant.

1. On a scale of 1 to 10 (10 being best), how good is your ability to manage money?

If both are below a 6 or 7, they should seek additional financial guidance. Two excellent resources you can refer to your couple to assist them in improving their money management skills are www.DaveRamsey.com and www.crown.org.

2. Will you have joint accounts, separate accounts, or both?

There is not a right or wrong to this. The main thing is that you discuss it and agree upon it. Transparency with your income and spending is very important. Using a free tool like Mint.com is a great way to ensure transparency with your money matters as well as give you an overview of your all your finances.

3. **Which one of you will pay the bills? Why?**

Whichever one of you is most responsible should be the one who ultimately makes sure that the bills are paid every month. However, finances should be a team effort. Plan a time every month to sit down together as a team to review your budget. Both of you should be fully aware of your financial situation.

4. **Fill in the blank. I think any *discretionary* purchase over the following amount should require the agreement of both the husband and the wife:**

$_____

It is not so important what this amount is as that you both agree on an amount. One thing to keep in mind is that you will value things differently. One of you may put a high value on buying clothes. The other one may put more value on buying computer games.

Remember that discretionary spending is not for necessities. It is optional, fun spending that is done with extra money after your obligations are met. You will probably have different ways you will want to spend your extra money.

5. **Identify an area where your fiancé spends money for which you don't understand the value or importance.**

A wife may have trouble understanding why her husband spends $100 for a computer game. Likewise, a husband may not understand why his wife spends $100 on a purse. Neither one of these is wrong provided you can afford the purchases. It is most important to make purchases that are within budget and not impulsive. Recognize that you will likely have different ways you will each want to spend discretionary income. Provided it fits into your budget, be understanding of your differences.

6. **If you received a sweepstakes cash award of $50,000, what would you recommend you do with it as a couple?**

7. **What do you believe your current FICO score is? Your partner's?**

   FICO scores range between 350 and 850. An average FICO score is around 680 and anything above 720 is considered excellent. If you are unaware of your current FICO score, you can obtain it online for free at www.CreditKarma.com. Your FICO score is a good indicator of how well you are managing your finances and plays a big part in attaining financing for big purchases such as a home. Always paying your bills on time and not maximizing your credit lines are two key factors that play into achieving a good score.

8. **What is your biggest concern for your future finances as a couple?**

9. **Complete an Annual Budget and a Financial Statement of Net Worth together *with* your fiancé. You can use the guides on the following pages to assist you.**

   Make sure that your couple completed their "Monthly Budget" and "Financial Statement of Worth" together. Depending on your financial abilities, you may feel comfortable reviewing these forms with your couple, or you may prefer to limit your comments. Encourage your couple to continue being a student of finances by enrolling in either a Dave Ramsey class or a Crown Ministries course. These are often offered at local churches.

   • Do you have questions on chapter sixteen?

CHAPTER 17

Marriage Goals

1. **What Bible verse would you like to commit to memory this year? This verse should focus on helping you improve one area in your life.**

   Imagine how much personal improvement will take place if you memorize a new verse each year.

2. **List some of your ideas for goals in the following areas:**

Type of Goal	Goal Ideas
Spiritual	
Time with each other	

Type of Goal	Goal Ideas
Family	
Vacation	You will likely be going on a honeymoon your first year. It is important to schedule vacation time together every year. Remember, you don't have to leave town to have a vacation.
Personal	
Health and fitness	Commit to taking good care of your health as a gift to your partner.

3. **Make a date with your fiancé to develop goals as a couple for the next year. Write the specific date, time, and place below.**

• Do you have any questions on chapter seventeen?

CHAPTER 18

Keeping the Flame Going

- Make sure your couple sets a date to review the 21 questions below.

Mentor note: The twenty-one questions and explanations from the workbook begin on the next page.

TWENTY-ONE QUESTIONS

1. **Are all three types of love (eros, philia, and agape) present in your marriage?**

   Review the list you wrote of ten things you love about your fiancé in chapter 2. Discuss together how you can each express the three types of love towards each other more fully. Keep this list available and refer to it often. Whenever you become discouraged about your marriage, re-read the list of things you love about your partner. One of the most effective tools for overcoming marital disappointment is replacing a negative thought about your husband or wife with thoughts of gratitude. Studies show that we can focus on only one emotion at a time: choose love. (Refer to chapter 2.)

2. **Have you both forgiven each other for everything?**

   Make sure forgiveness flows freely between you and your spouse for conflicts both BIG and small. Practice forgiving, not collecting, hurts. God has forgiven us for all of our sins. He wants us to forgive one another freely. "Bear with each other and forgive whatever grievances you may have against one another. Forgive as the Lord forgave you" (Colossians 3:13). We forgive by faith, out of obedience to God. God wants us to love others and to love Him. This love He speaks of is a choice, not a feeling. We must trust God to complete His work in us. Make it between you and God and not between you and your spouse. Turn your heart over to God. Corrie ten Boom, a Christian who survived a Nazi concentration camp, said, "Forgiveness is the key that unlocks the door of resentment and the handcuffs of hatred. It is a power that breaks the chains of bitterness and the shackles of selfishness."[3] One of the most loving actions you can continually take is forgiving. (Refer to chapter 3.)

---

[3] Corrie ten Boom, *Clippings from My Notebook*, (Nashville: Thomas Nelson, 1982), 19.

3. **Are you living out the biblical roles outlined for a husband and wife in Ephesians 5:21–33?**

We each need to worshipfully surrender our lives to Christ. Ultimately, a wife answers to God for how well she submits to her husband's leadership, whether or not he is making good, loving decisions. Ultimately, a husband answers to God for how well he loves his wife, regardless of whether or not she respects and submits to him.

When your spouse falls short of living out God's will in your marriage, take your frustrations to God. Trust God to meet your needs, and he will fill you with his love to take back into the marriage. In doing this, instead of expecting perfect behavior from two imperfect people, you look for the perfect response from your perfect God. (Refer to chapter 4.)

4. **Are you continuing to pray together often?**

If not, set a time at least once a week to pray together. Remember, God wants to bless your marriage beyond your imagination, but you need to invite Him in and follow His will together. There is nothing more important than keeping God at the center of your marriage. (Refer to chapter 4.)

5. **Do you continue to share specifically with your spouse how he or she can pray for you?**

Prayer is one of the most loving, intimate expressions that can be exchanged between a husband and wife. After you share your prayer requests with each other, pray out loud together for each other. (Refer to chapter 4.)

6. **Is your spouse meeting your most important wants and needs?**

You may desire a weekly date night; time to talk about light topics; fun together doing a hobby; more frequent sex; more transparency with the finances; more home cooking; staying physically fit; entertaining more with family and friends; hearing more affirming statements; having more intimate, open, honest conversations; etc. Share your desires in a loving way with your spouse.

We should not look to our spouse to make us happy. There will be times in your marriage when it will be more profitable to take the focus off of your partner meeting your wants and onto God. Philippians 4:19 assures us, "God will meet all your needs according to his glorious riches in Christ Jesus." Bob and Judy Hughes' book, *Love Focused*, is an excellent resource to understand this concept better. They also have a couples Bible study you could do together. (Refer to chapter 5.)

7. **Have you established a weekly King for the Day and Queen for the Day?**

   Share with each other what you would like for your spouse to do for you on your day. Be attentive to meeting your spouse's wishes on his or her day. Remember, this can be a real game-changer! (Refer to chapter 5.)

8. **Are there any areas in which you feel your spouse is not successfully fulfilling his or her role in marriage?**

   God gives specific instructions for husbands to love their wives as Christ loved the church. God instructs wives to respect their husbands and submit to their leadership in the family. Lovingly discuss any areas you would like to see improved, and share what betterment looks like to you. (Refer to chapter 5.)

9. **Are you spending most of your time in the sweet spot?**

   A marriage has momentum in the direction of the sweet spot or the sour patch. If you are not spending the majority of your time in the sweet spot, go back and review the eighteen skills for staying in the sweet spot. Remember, fun is the litmus test of a good relationship. Do something fun together. (Refer to chapter 6.)

10. Are you dealing effectively with your incompatibilities?

A great marriage is not based on marrying someone compatible, because God does not make any two people perfectly compatible; it is based on learning how to deal effectively with your incompatibilities. If you are struggling with compatibility, consider taking a Myers-Briggs Type Indicator® instrument to identify your personality styles (http://www.16personalities.com offers a free test online). Remember there is not a right or wrong to personality differences. You are both created in the image of God. Work on becoming more understanding and accepting of the fact that you approach life differently. (Refer to chapter 7.)

11. Are the differences between men and women causing friction in your marriage?

Men and women have very different operating systems. We will never completely understand each other, but we can educate ourselves on what is important to each other. God wants our differences to complement and complete each other in marriage as we work together as one. (Refer to chapter 8.)

12. On a scale of 1 to 10, how full is your love tank? What can your spouse do to make it a 10?

Remember to speak to your spouse in his or her love language, and remind your spouse to talk to you in your language. You may want to read the book, *The Five Love Languages*, by Gary Chapman. (Refer to chapter 9.)

13. Are there any issues with your family relationships that are causing problems in your marriage?

Discuss what you can do to improve any family tension. Be sure that your relationship with each other is kept primary and that you always show a united front. When problems arise with your family, face them together. Discuss them together as husband and wife. Pray about them together. If needed, seek outside counsel from trusted advisors or professionals. Finally, keep things in perspective. Don't major in minors. If it is not going to be life altering for your child, natural consequences may be the best teacher. If extended family members are causing issues, sometimes it is best to set healthy boundaries to protect your primary family relationships. (Refer to chapter 10.)

14. Are you communicating with each other effectively?

Content, tone, and body language are all important aspects of communication, but listening and choosing the appropriate time for sensitive conversations are also important. Work on any weaknesses in your communication. When couples are having trouble with communication, it is often a symptom of a bigger issue. Try to identify the bigger issue and work that through with the other tools offered through this program (such as the "Ten Rules to Resolve Conflict" in appendix 7). Above all, always speak to each other in love using the rules for discussion. (Refer to chapter 11.)

15. Do you have any unresolved conflict in your marriage?

Conflicts come in all shapes and sizes. With moderate conflicts, use the Start or Stop and Continue Method. If you have a major conflict, set a time to use the "Ten Rules to Resolve Conflict" in appendix 7 to resolve your conflict. (Refer to chapter 12.)

16. Are you enjoying the emotional intimacy you desire with your spouse?

You should feel comfortable and safe sharing your most intimate thoughts and dreams with each other. It is as if you are saying, "into-me-see." Growing in this area involves a continual effort and investment in your relationship. (Refer to chapter 13.)

17. Do you have a vibrant sex life?

If your love life isn't all that you would like it to be, the best way to revitalize your physical intimacy is to communicate openly and honestly with each other. Truthfully communicate your desires to your spouse. Be sensitive and loving in fulfilling your partner's wishes. Try something fun like showering together. (Refer to chapter 14.)

18. **Is your marriage safely affair-proofed?**

It's too late to prevent an affair after it's happened. Protect your marriage by keeping proper boundaries in place. It is especially important to give each other full access to all of your communication devices and your social networking sites. Discuss if there are any areas that need to be reinforced. (Refer to chapter 15.)

19. **Are your finances healthy?**

Be transparent with each other with your spending. Recognize that you will likely have different ways you will each want to spend discretionary income. Provided it fits into your budget, be understanding of your differences. A budget and financial statement are good ways to keep on track with your finances. A helpful tool for creating a budget and maintaining transparency with your finances is https://www.mint.com. If you need some extra guidance on your finances, many churches offer financial counseling following either Dave Ramsey's principles or Crown Ministries. Find information on these programs at www.daveramsey.com and www.crown.org. (Refer to chapter 16.)

20. **Have you set goals together as a couple?**

One of the cornerstones to this program is having an intentional marriage. Relationships are either getting better or getting worse. They don't stay the same. It is important to continue pursuing goals and dreams as a couple. In order for this to happen you need to set goals and take action steps. In order for goals to truly take hold they should be written down and reviewed for progress. (Refer to Chapter 17.)

21. **Are you involved in a small group for couples?**

Fellowship with other believers is one of the conduits God uses to share His truth with us. Communing with other Christian married couples will help enrich your marriage through shared life experiences and godly insights. (Refer to chapter 17.)

Please discuss the answer to the following question together before you meet with your mentor couple.

1. **In taking inventory on your relationship today using the questions above, which areas did you identify as still needing growth? Be honest. Please list the numbers of those questions.**

2. **Decide the dates for your quarterly marriage assessment and tune-up. Write the dates below.**

- Any questions on chapter 18?

Closing Comments

- Your premarital counseling is now complete. This program was designed to give you God's blueprint so you would know the actions to take in order to experience a joyful marriage. You will need to make a commitment to intentionally continue investing in your relationship. One final comment: remember to keep the main thing, the main thing. What is the main thing? **Keep Christ at the center of your marriage.**

- All hold hands and pray out loud together. We suggest designating that the male mentor will close out the prayer.

CPSIA information can be obtained
at www.ICGtesting.com
Printed in the USA
LVHW101136100720
660315LV00010B/165